PINK vision board CLIP ART BOOK

400+ elements
BY KALISHIA WINSTON

DOWNLOAD INCLUDED ➤

🎁 YOUR FREE GIFTS

As a token of appreciation for your purchase, I'm excited to offer you four valuable bonuses:

#1: "Creating Your Dream Life with Your Own Vision Board" (Course)

Unlock the potential within you and start manifesting your aspirations with my exclusive vision board course. Set clear intentions and turn your dreams into reality.

#2: "86 Quick & Easy Strategies for Saving Money" (eBook)

Discover 86 practical and easy-to-implement strategies to save money, budget wisely, and achieve your financial goals. This eBook is an indispensable guide for securing your financial future.

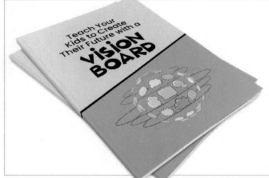

#3: "Teach Your Kids to Create Their Future with a Vision Board" (eBook)

Unlock the potential within you and start manifesting your aspirations with my exclusive vision board course. Set clear intentions and turn your dreams into reality.

To access the first three gifts, sign up for my email newsletter for instant access at pink.kalishiawinston.com. Alongside these gifts, you will also receive tips, free book giveaways, discounts, and so much more.

#4 "Pink Vision Board Clip Art Book" (Printable PDF)

Inside the Pink Vision Board Clip Art Book, you'll find a treasure trove of inspiring clip art elements to fuel your dreams and creativity. But what if you need extra copies for a vision board party or want to retry cutting out an element? No worries!

Simply enter the link to access the PDF file, ready for printing (no email sign-up required): pink-pdf.kalishiawinston.com

All of these bonuses are completely free and come with no strings attached. For the first three gifts, you only need to provide your email address. Enjoy your free gifts, and here's to achieving your dreams!

find your **BALANCE**

YOGA

mindfulness

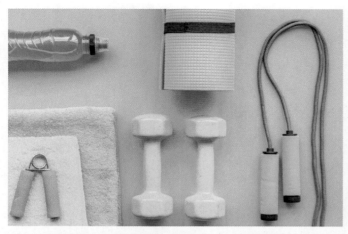

RUNNING

WEIGHT LOSS

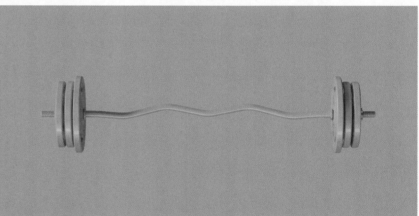

TRAIN HARD FITNESS

STUDY ABROAD

E-LEARNING

LEARN NEW SKILLS

INVEST IN KNOWLEDGE

Podcast

GRADUATION EDUCATION

MARRIED

LOVE

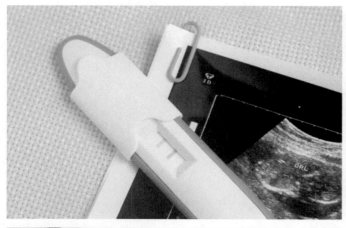

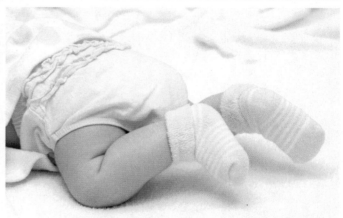

Baby Shower **I'M PREGNANT!** ♥

GAME NIGHT

" LIFE IS BETTER WITH TRUE FRIENDS "

FRIENDSHIP   SUPPORT EACH OTHER

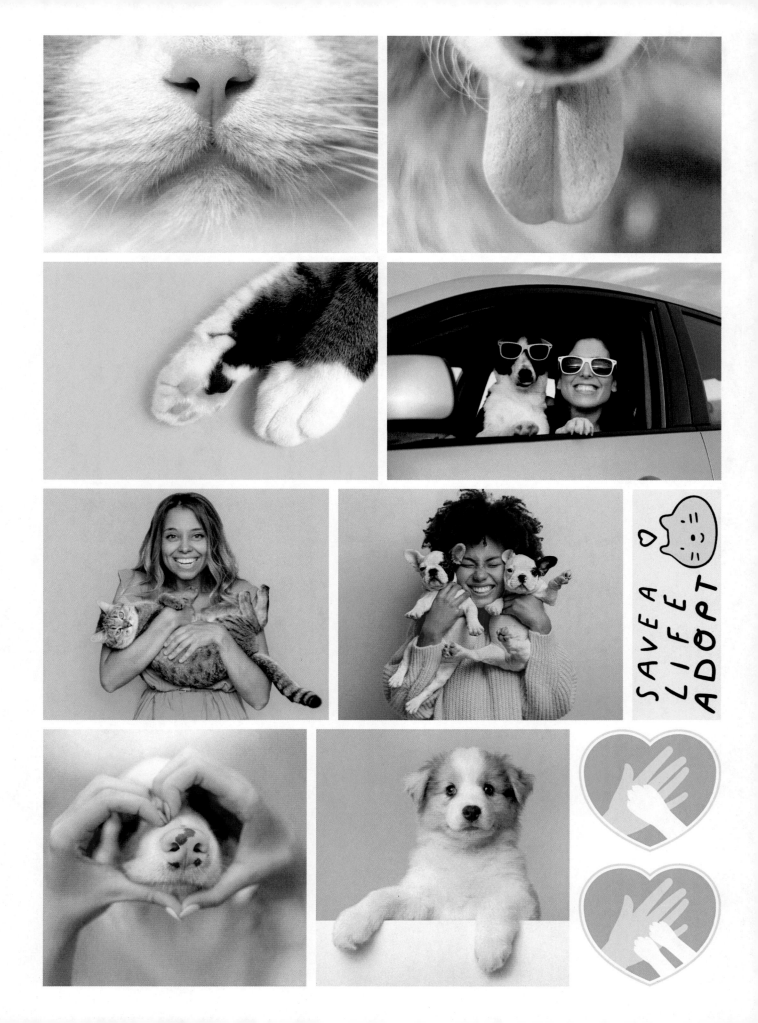

SAVE A
LIFE
ADOPT

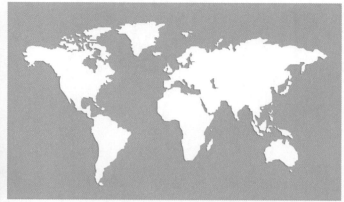

TRAVELER

RIO DE JANEIRO

LISBON

ROME

MANAROLA
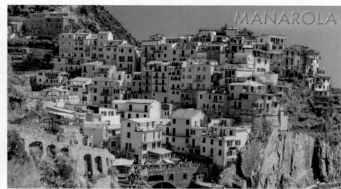

VENICE

LONDON

SANTORINI

PARIS

EGYPT
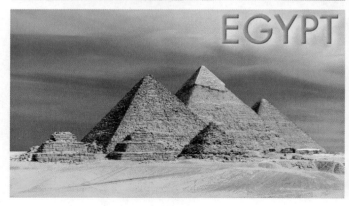

ATHENS

CANCUN

CHICHEN ITZA

DOMINICAN REPUBLIC

MALDIVES

CANADA

TORONTO

AFRICA

BARCELONA

DUBAI

CROATIA

GREAT WALL OF CHINA

#GIRLBOSS

Make More Money!

DECIDE. COMMIT. SUCCEED.

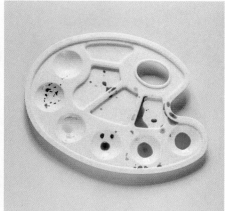

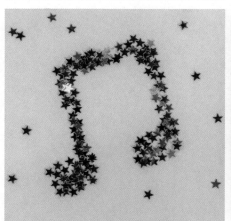

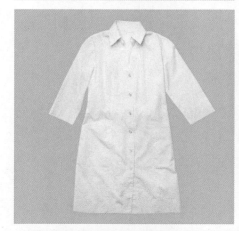
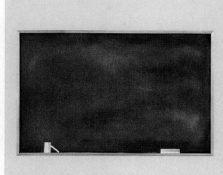

I LOVE MY JOB Passion

GARDENING

PHOTOGRAPHY

PAINTING

KNITTING

WOODWORKING

POTTERY

COOKING

BAKING

DRAWING

WRITING

PLAYING GUITAR

SINGING

PIANO PLAYING

DIY PROJECTS

JOURNALING

BLOGGING

BIRD WATCHING

FISHING

ASTRONOMY

DANCING

DIGITAL ART

PODCASTING

SCRAPBOOKING

MODEL BUILDING

BOARD GAMES

UPCYCLING

OMG!

I LOST

....

POUNDS!

Digital Detox

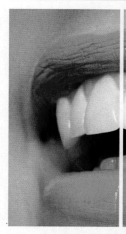

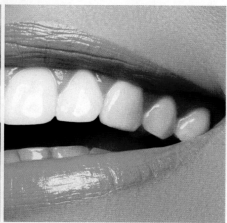

GET ENOUGH
SLEEP

SELF ♡ CARE

MoRe SOCIAL Less MEDIA

self care ISN'T SELFISH

LOVE YOURSELF More. SELF CARE matters MAKE YOURSELF a Priority

DREAM HOME ECOHOUSE

PRIVATE JET

YACHT

MILLIONAIRE | Abundance

CAREER	BU$INE$$	LEADERSHIP
CREATIVITY	WEALTH	GOALS
INNOVATION	FUN	HEALTH
WELLNESS	FINANCE	SAVINGS
SPIRITUALITY	MINDSET	FAMILY
EMPOWERMENT	HOBBIES	PERSONAL GROWTH
MANIFEST	SCHOOL	HARMONY
GIVING BACK	ACHIEVEMENT	EXPLORATION
PETS	MENTAL HEALTH	COMMUNITY
ADVENTURE	KIDS	FAITH
LIFESTYLE	SELF LOVE	GRATITUDE
CONNECTION	RESILIENCE	BALANCE

THINGS TO SEE	FOCUS	LUXURY
DREAM JOB	INDEPENDENT	PROGRESS
SUCCESSFUL	MY DREAM LIFE	BELIEVE
WEDDING	GOALS TO MEET	TAKE RISKS
DREAMER	LESS SCREEN TIME	STUDY
THRIVE	CALM	UNLEASH POTENTIAL
EVERY DAY	CREATE	LIVE SIMPLY
PROFIT	THINGS TO TRY	LOVE YOUR LIFE
EXPERIENCES	BEAUTIFUL	OUTDOORS
IMAGINE	HOPE	GRATEFUL
JOY	GET IT	GREATNESS
GROW	HAPPINESS	ASPIRE HIGHER

I set and honor my boundaries to protect my energy.

I don't wait for others to give me the love I deserve. I love me.

I recognize my power and strength.

I forgive myself for the past and embrace my present self.

I speak positive words to myself every day.

I am so much more than just a physical body.

I embrace my feminine energy.

I allow myself to receive love.

I am in awe of how amazing I truly am.

I can do anything I put my mind to.

I am beautiful inside and out.

I am the best version of myself.

I am happy
AND COMPLETE
today and forever.

There is a
Power for good
in the universe
greater than
I AM AND I CAN USE IT!

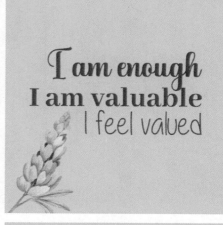

I am enough
I am valuable
I feel valued

I love God
and
GOD LOVES ME.

The Universe
is for me
and with me.

I am a
Rich
BLESSING TO ALL

I am beautiful
loving and powerful
RIGHT NOW

I am
the consciousness
of success attracting
SUCCESS

I am the
BEST
IN MY WORLD.

I am beautiful
loving and powerful
RIGHT NOW.

I am happy
and complete
today and forever

I deserve
AND
ACCEPT THE BEST

AMSTERDAM	ARUBA	ASIA
ATLANTA	AUSTRALIA	BAHAMAS
BALI	BANFF	BANGKOK
BERLIN	BORA BORA	BOSTON
BUENOS AIRES	CALIFORNIA	CHINA
CUBA	DALLAS	DENMARK
DENVER	DUBLIN	EL SALVADOR
EUROPE	FIJI	FLORIDA
FRANCE	GERMANY	GREECE
HAWAII	HONG KONG	HOUSTON
INDIA	IRELAND	ISTANBUL

JAMAICA	JORDAN	LISBON
MEXICO	MICHIGAN	MOROCCO
NEPAL	NEW ZEALAND	NORWAY
ORLANDO	PENNSYLVANIA	PERU
PHILIPPINES	PHOENIX	POLAND
PORTUGAL	PRAGUE	PUERTO RICO
SCOTLAND	SEATTLE	SEOUL
SOUTH AMERICA	SOUTH KOREA	SPAIN
SWEDEN	SWITZERLAND	THAILAND
TOKYO	TULUM	TURKEY
UNITED KINGDOM	USA	VIETNAM

BOARDING PASS

PASSENGER NAME: DESTINATION:

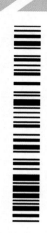

TIME: DATE:

For manifesting purposes only. Not for use to board a flight at the airport.

🏛 **BANK OF THE UNIVERSE**   3639

DATE _____

PAY TO THE
ORDER OF _____ $ [_____]

_____ DOLLARS 🔒

MEMO _____   _____

For manifesting purposes only.   ''161914353'' 454833i: 6538 92

TICKET

ADMIT ONE

DATE:

EVENT: EXLUSIVELY FOR:

LOCATION:

For the sole purpose of manifesting your desires.

BECOMING my BEST SELF

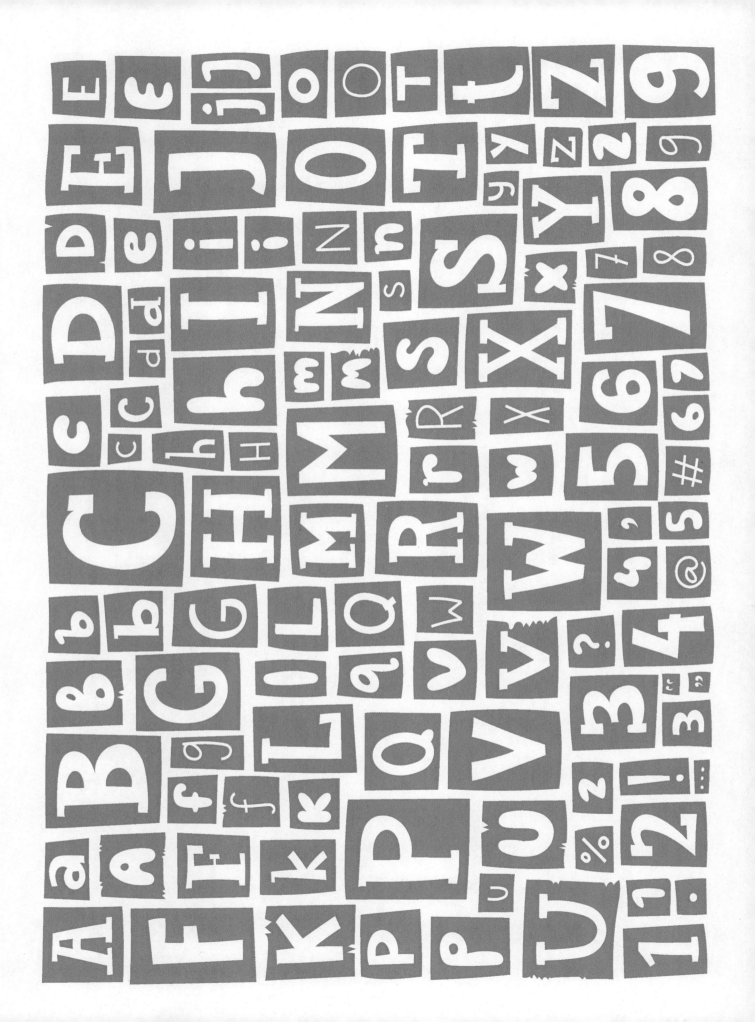

Thank You!

> "*Helping others is the way we help ourselves.*"
>
> -Oprah Winfrey

Have you ever given without expecting anything in return? If you have, you are aware of the tremendous rewards that can come from helping others. Not because it makes you a better person, but because it makes you feel good to know that you were able to improve someone else's life in some small way.

I want to give you this chance and ask you for a favor. In order for me to accomplish my mission of inspiring my readers to live their best lives, I first have to reach them. And the majority of people do evaluate a book based on its reviews. So, could you please take 3 minutes to post your honest review of this book on Amazon? With your help, this book will reach more people and assist them in achieving their goals and dreams. Just find this book on Amazon and write a few short words (or long words, I won't judge).

P.S. If you believe this book will benefit someone you know, please let them know about it too.

To your success,

Kalishia Winston

Made in the USA
Las Vegas, NV
19 April 2024

88877462R00033